FAITH LESSONS FOR LITTLE ONES – VOLUME 1
Copyright © 2023 by Spirit & Truth

For information contact :
SPIRIT & TRUTH
PO BOX 1737
MARTINSVILLE, IN 46151
spiritandtruthonline.org

Book and Cover design by Ghyvari Medie Ben
ISBN: 978-1-0881-1167-3

First Edition: April 2022

10 9 8 7 6 5 4 3 2 1

The Creation
(Genesis 1)

In the beginning, God made the world. But then it
turned dark and empty, so God said, "Let there be Light!"
Then He made heaven and dry Land, plants, stars and
planets, and animals too. But God wasn't finished yet!
He wanted a family...so then He made people like us!
We are made in God's image, and God says "That's good!"

Thank you, God, for making us Your family!

Adam & Eve
(Genesis 2-3)

God made the first people, Adam and Eve, to be His family and take care of His creation. But Adam and Eve were tricked by a being so wicked, God called him a "snake"! He was really a fallen angel who was against God and wanted to break what God loved. So he tricked God's family, Adam and Eve listened to him instead of God, and God had to put a special plan in place to fix what they broke.

Thank you, God, for loving us so much You made a plan to fix the world!

Noah & The Flood
(Genesis 6–8)

The world wasn't a happy place. People only wanted to disobey and do bad things God said not to. So God told Noah, the only person who obeyed Him, to build a boat called an ark. He sent animals to Noah—seven pairs each of the clean animals and one pair each of the unclean ones. Once they were all on board, God closed the ark doors. Then it rained so hard, the whole world flooded! But Noah's family and the animals on the ark survived. When it was safe, they left the ark to start a new life. God put the first rainbow in the sky as a sign He would never flood the world again.

Thank you, God, for keeping Your people safe even in bad times!

Joseph
(Genesis 37–50)

There was a boy named Joseph who had eleven brothers. They were really important to God's plans to fix the world, but they got mad that Joseph was their father's favorite, so they gave him away and hid it from their family! But God was with Joseph in his new home, Egypt. After lots of hard times, Joseph was put in charge of almost the whole kingdom! When there was no food in the land, his brothers came to Joseph's new home for something to eat, and he forgave them and helped keep their family alive.

Thank you, God, for making good things happen even when they start off bad!

Moses
(The Book of Exodus)

Moses was a special baby born during a special time. God's people were forced to serve Egypt's cruel leader, the Pharoah, but God had a plan to save them...with Moses! Moses ran away from Egypt and spent a long time living in the desert before God told him to save His people. God did lots of miracles through Moses to try and stop the cruelty, but the Pharoah's heart stayed hard. Finally, when God's judgement became too much, the Pharoah let Moses and his people go. Moses took them into the desert toward the land God had promised them so they could serve Him!

Thank you, God, for making us part of
Your plans to fix the world!

King David
(1&2 Samuel, 1&2 Chronicles, Psalms)

God's people wanted a king, but the one they had was disobedient. So God chose a new king—a shepherd boy named David. It took a long time for David to become king, but during that time he fought God's enemies, protected the people, and wrote lots of songs called psalms about his experiences. Finally, David took the throne and led God's people. He wasn't perfect, and he made some bad choices, but God still called him "A man after My own heart." He even made David's family part of His plans to fix the world!

Thank You, God, for loving us and forgiving us when we make mistakes and helping us be better!

Jonah & The Great Fish
(The Book of Jonah)

God sent a man named Jonah to save the city of Nineveh.
But Jonah knew from men and women God spoke to that
saving Nineveh would be trouble for his people, so he ran
instead! He tried to sail away, but God stopped him with a
storm. Jonah told the people on the boat to throw him
overboard, where a big fish swallowed him up! For three
days and three nights, Jonah was dead inside the fish. Then
God made it spit him out! God brought Jonah back to life,
and Jonah finally went to Nineveh. Its people stopped
their wicked ways, but Jonah was angry. He didn't want
them to be spared! God reminded Jonah that those were
real lives that mattered to Him, too.

Thank you, God, for keeping us honest
and humble before You!

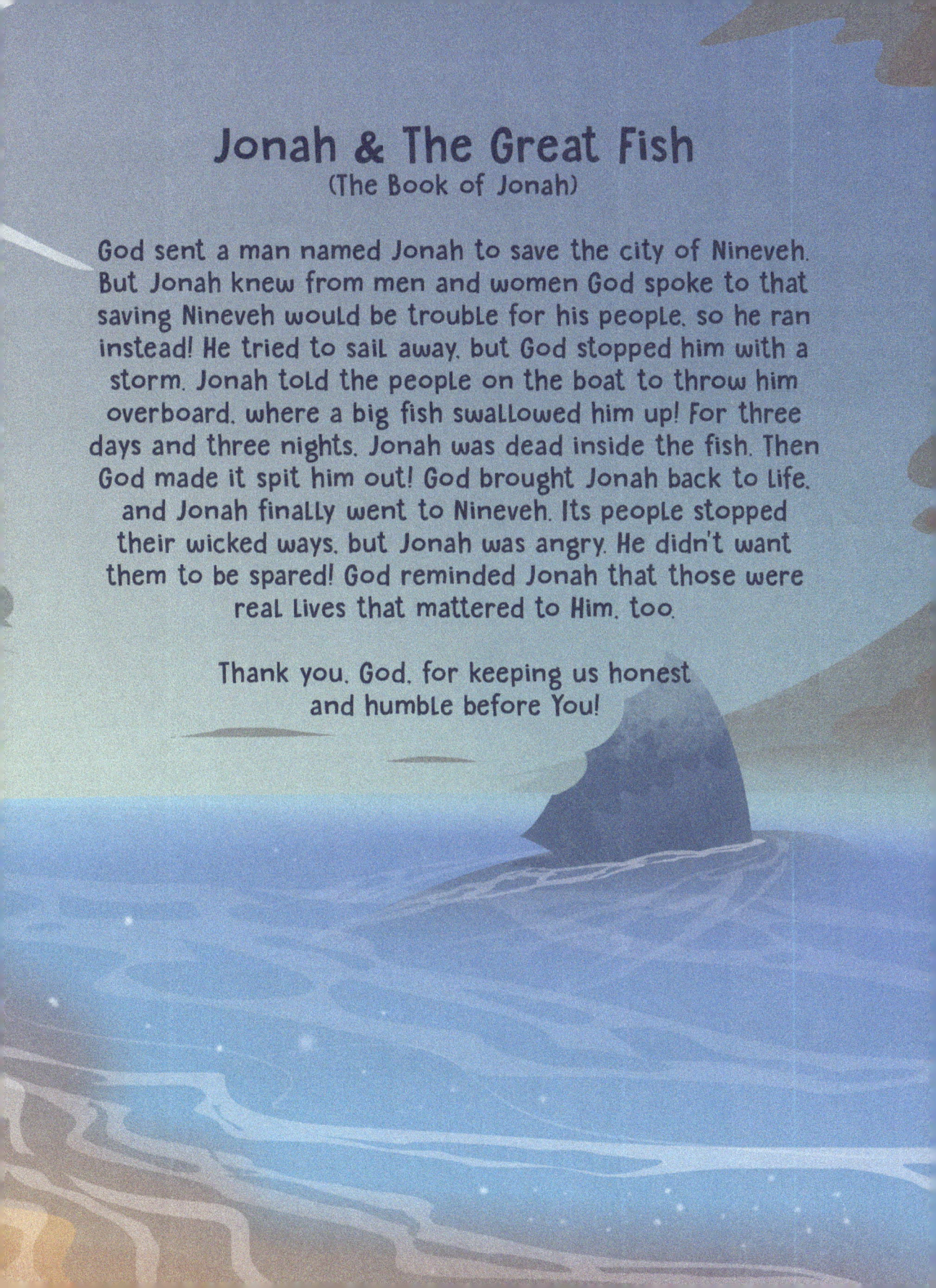

The Birth of Jesus
(Matthew 1, Luke 2)

There was a girl named Mary, one of King David's descendants, who was engaged to a man named Joseph. God created life in Mary—a baby who would be called Jesus, the Son of God! Mary and Joseph took a long journey to their hometown, and they stayed with family there. When Jesus was born, they laid him in a feeding box for the animals, who stayed in the house at night. Then angels came to tell shepherds nearby about the birth. The shepherds came to the house, and everyone celebrated the birth of Jesus together!

Thank You, God, for the birth of Your wonderful Son, Jesus!

The Magi Visit Jesus
(Matthew 2)

When Jesus was a little boy, about two years old, a whole group of men from a faraway kingdom came to see him! They followed ancient stories about a future King to find where he would be, and brought him gifts like spices. But they had to go home on a different road because the King in charge in those days was afraid of the story about a different future King. He wanted to stop Jesus from ever growing up, so he attacked all the little boys Jesus's age and younger; but angels warned Joseph, and their family went to a different kingdom so Jesus could grow up safely. His life touched other places, too!

Thank you, God, for making it so people everywhere can meet Your Son!

Jesus's Ministry
(The Gospels)

When Jesus was grown up, God called him to spread the good news about the kingdom of God. He reached people's hearts with stories, miracles, and lots of teachings. There were people who wanted to stop him because they didn't want things to change, but Jesus kept doing God's will...even when it was the hardest thing he ever had to do! God rewarded his faithfulness by raising him from the dead and giving him power and authority to lead God's family. This was the plan God put in place to fix the world...and Jesus finished it!

Thank you, God, for sending Jesus to fix the world!

Pentecost
(Acts 2)

After Jesus was taken alive up to be God's helper in Heaven, his friends weren't quite sure what to do next. But then, one day when they were all gathered together, something like a big wind filled the place where they were, and tongues of fire came on their shoulders. Then they started speaking languages from all over the world! This was the gift of holy spirit, a piece of God's power in each of them. And there's a piece in everyone who follows Jesus today! That power is proof that we're saved and part of God's family, and we can use it to help people and bring them into the family, too!

Thank You, God, for sharing Your power with everyone in Your family!

The Good News Spreads
(Acts 8 to Today)

God shared His holy spirit with His family, but it was just as hard for them to talk about God's plans as it had been for Jesus. People tried to stop them from talking about who Jesus was and what God did for them. The evil people even hurt Jesus's followers to keep them quiet! But the Good News about God's Kingdom and Jesus's resurrection kept spreading through many people who risked everything to carry it all around the world. That's how we have it today! Now we get to help spread it so people everywhere have the chance to be saved!

Thank You, God, for making the Good News spread so everyone has a chance to be part of Your family!

www.ingramcontent.com/pod-product-compliance
Lightning Source LLC
Chambersburg PA
CBHW060755150426

42811CB00058B/1416

she

A collection of you, me, her

she

A collection of you, me, her

Tiare Snow

the kind press

First published by the kind press, 2020

Illustrations: Rebecca Ivkovich

Cover and interior design: Elle Lynn

Cataloguing-in-Publication entry is available from the National Library Australia.

NATIONAL
LIBRARY
OF AUSTRALIA

ISBN: 978-0-6487927-0-3 (Hardback)

Dedicated to

my mum.

For being the voice of reason when I often lose my own.

For never wavering in your belief of my existence.

For laughing at all my jokes (I'm hilarious).

For reading all my words.

Preface

A journey through time divided into four major female roles.

The wanderer: finding herself in newfound freedoms

The lover: moulding her heart by way of trial and error

The mother: becoming a new version of herself

The wonderer: she is not finished yet

Contents

Preface   vii

THE WANDERER

School's Out   3

Map   5

Mexico   7

A Romance Novel   9

By The Time   11

Desperate Measures   13

Facade   15

Reality Cheque   17

Bad Behaviour   19

Just   21

THE LOVER

Bus Love   25

Love   27

My Ocean   29

Table Talk   31

A Spoonful   33

Divorce   35

Rough Draft   37

Identity Theft   39

Murder   41

Floating   43

THE MOTHER

Apple   47

Mornings   49

Showers   51

Swim   53

Change   55

One Act   57

Clean   59

Flash   61

Crust   63

Mother Earth   65

THE WONDERER

All The Things   69

Fuel   71

Displaced   73

Wonder   75

Dawn   77

Running   79

Clay   81

Got the look   83

All out   85

Strut   87

About the author   90

The Wanderer

In school she had it all: the safety of routine.
Years spent being told what she should wear,
where she should go, and what she should do,
only to be shown the door and asked, 'What are
you going to do now?'

She wandered off onto footpaths with no signage,
walking in and out of jobs, bars, broken hearts.
She wandered around in her twenties trying to
figure out where she was going, and what she was
going to be.

School's Out

No longer constricted by her school noose,

but rather

free

to experiment with a loosened tie;

she sticks her neck out.

Map

Stripped from her tangible happiness,

she found herself without and wanting.

The void became a gaping hole inside her chest,

her mind,

her soul.

She followed the ache like dots on a map

in search of unknown treasure

wishing to drape her in purpose.

Little did she know

she was the X that marked the spot.

She had to dig within.

Mexico

Her skin melted into the sand.

She drank

as though from the fountain of youth;

it was.

Her days were blue oceans kissing sunburnt skies.

Her nights were liqueurs dancing against sweaty tomorrows.

She was ever-present, effervescent.

She was Mexico.

A Romance Novel

She wrote a love story on tissue paper.

She wiped away her tears with every word.

By The Time

Her ponytail loosened with a single sip.

By the end of her first glass, she had completely let her hair down.

She wore the tie around her wrist to prove it.

Desperate Measures

She rolled herself in double-sided tape,

webbed her fingers with mesh and smeared

glue under her feet.

She screwed hooks into her back,

latched loops over her fingertips,

strung webs across her body.

And stood,

arms wide towards the world,

she waited

desperately yet

patiently.

She was just trying to catch a break.

Façade

She glued diamantes to her eyelids,

painted glitter in her lipstick;

all an attempt to distract from her personality.

She turned her face into artwork

until she could figure out a way

to glue diamantes to her attitude

and glitter paint to her disposition.

Reality Cheque

She dipped her glossy toes in rent and utilities.

It chipped the paint.

Bad Behaviour

She made plans with name-calling and tear jerking.

She was bought with a cheap ring and empty promises.

She thought it would be her last love.

She would not know, for many years to come,

that it was not even her first.

Just

She is just a girl.

A girl whose journey in the beginning

will be paved

with shards of glass,

broken hearts

and empty wine bottles.

There will be hurt before joy

and when the joy does come,

the hurt will be replaced

with an awareness

that questions

her insecurities

and makes room for personal growth.

She will never again be *just* a girl.

The Lover

To love and to be loved was her instinctual desire.
Her journey, so far, had tricked her into
believing that love was breaking up and making
up. She had a way to go.
She hadn't yet experienced a love that kept her
sane, safe and celebrated. When she did, she
didn't fall down a rabbit hole or get hit with an
arrow. She woke up to her unhealthy learned
behaviours and allowed herself to accept a love
deserving of her worth.

Bus Love

She hoped the bus would break down,

leaving them to hold hands just a little longer.

True love hid behind their words,

their eyes questioning each other.

A lifetime of happiness rested palm to palm but

time had them parting ways.

They would hold onto memories of squeezed knees

and stomach butterflies

until the clock landed on their perfect timing.

Love

She dips him in chocolate,

he is her strawberry.

She sips him from a long-stemmed glass,

he is her champagne.

She gives him space to watch him grow,

he is her garden.

She risks it all,

he is her heart.

My Ocean

She often wondered if he feared that she would return to the ocean.

She felt him twitch in his sleep, as she lay awake hoping

he wasn't dreaming of the glitter on her tail.

She rubs her feet together and feels where her scales were once soft,

hard nails now where her tasselled fins would once tickle each other.

She rests her head on his chest and breathes his heartbeat.

She twists her ankles around his as a reminder that she is beside him.

She whispers in his ear a song that will ease his terror, *My love,*

you are my ocean.

Table Talk

It's not all silence at the table.

The knives and forks are at it again,

slicing,

clanking,

swearing metal profanities.

She doesn't usually notice their bickering,

but tonight

they take the stage while the curtain seems drawn on her own.

A Spoonful

On this particular day,

she chose to spread honey on her toast,

for she did not foresee herself

getting any sweeter otherwise.

Divorce

If he took her for all he thought she was worth

he would end up with very little.

So she took him for all that he wasn't,

all that he promised to be and never was.

She walked away with it all.

A richer woman indeed.

Rough Draft

She wished she could write her love-life in pencil

and rub out any mistakes.

Identity Theft

She would give up her heart before her name.

No matter how hard she fell

in or out of love;

she would always know herself.

Murder

She refused to wear her heart on her sleeve

in fear of getting blood on her hands.

Floating

She carried the weight of the world on her shoulders.

He carried her in his arms.

Weightless in his embrace,

she had the strength to kiss his lips.

He too became weightless.

The Mother

Becoming a mother unlocked a part of herself she had never met. She came across new expectations of herself that she did not know if she could reach. She experienced new love and cried new tears.

She became weak and strong all in a day.

Showers were her washing machine and therapist.

Apple

She thought she saw Eve

this morning,

in her true image,

bare, human, Creator.

She stared back at her, with protruding belly

providing breasts

clear mind.

Her reflection was modern, no rippled water to skew her appearance.

Eve touched the glass and circled the reflection of her belly button.

She would eat a thousand apples more if this were to be her punishment.

Mornings

She is still dark in the mornings.

She puts on her warpaint under the light of a candle,

dresses for combat in the shadow of the lamppost

light looming through her window.

She waits

for the sun to rise,

for the battle to begin.

Showers

Water freckles slid across his tiny face; a minute of peace surrounded them both.

She held him against her as the water ran across their bodies,

eyelashes sticking together as he tried to blink through the shower of rain.

The many ways the day ahead could go ran through her tired mind.

She closed her eyes and let him scratch away at her skin and slap at her face.

Just five more minutes, she thought.

Let's just stay in here for five more minutes;

where we are both safe from each other,

with each other,

where the world cannot tell us what to do.

Swim

She put on her bikini.

It had been a while.

The Lycra grabbed at her skin like hungry sucker fish.

It made her feel hugged,

taught.

She strut to the pool as her fuller self;

as long as she kept a baby nearby, her excuse was well known.

She let her long hair down and approached the pool like it was an old boyfriend,

like a woman who'd forgotten about him.

And she swam.

Change

Vulnerability was growing on her.

A softer

translucent aura

knocking down the cage of shame and fear.

She replaced the word 'unnecessary' with 'understandable'.

She held out her hand rather than waiting for it to be taken.

She whispered mantras in her son's ear, giving him the space

and opportunity to explore his own desires—and to go for

them without judgement from himself—to carry with him

the worthiness

that envelops

his soul.

She took a step back so that she could take a step forward.

She accepted the time that had been lost and moved into a

time that is now.

And she changed.

One Act

She bustles effortlessly in the kitchen, loading her already prepared toddler meal in

the microwave while her newborn lies across her chest,

swaddled in her left arm, asleep.

A nipple splays openly under the baby's chin,

two glasses of wine swaddle themselves under her belt.

It was all one motion,

one scene.

Perhaps, it was all one act.

Clean

She scrubbed the day off her skin.

Falling to the floor like scraps from a bad meal,

moments of impatience,

anger,

frustration,

piled up, waiting to be thrown to the dogs.

Her skin smoothed and she calmed.

Water filled her pores creating pools of forgiveness.

Soap lathered up hope for tomorrow.

A cleaner version of herself was she.

Flash

She runs him a bath when she needs a minute.

He splashes in the running water and plays games with rubber toys.

But she forgets to take her minute, instead losing it to domesticity.

He comes out soft and pruned around the edges,

clean,

calm,

ready for another round of go, go, go.

All the while

she forgot to stop.

Crust

She always served herself the crust.

That flimsy last piece of the loaf,

thinned at the edges,

hole poked through the middle from roughhousing.

She watched her children tear into warm abundant toast,

crumbs spluttering from their tiny chewing mouths,

eating from the inside out,

nothing but the firm edges that once framed their

breakfast left lying on the plate.

The crust.

Meanwhile,

her piece disintegrated before even reaching her tongue.

Dry remnants replicating the same sustenance

as last night's sleep.

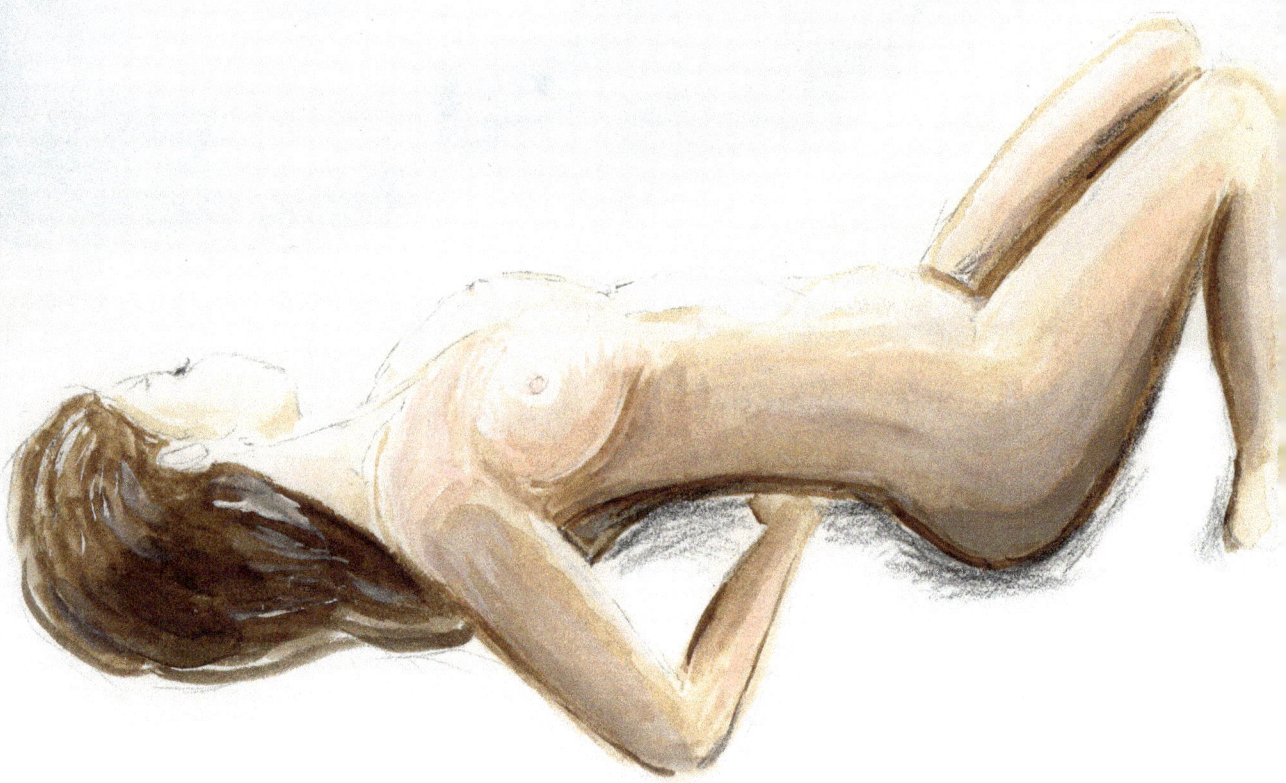

Mother Earth

She wanted to sky dive.

Fall towards the earth and rain down on her friends and

family in a roar of glory

to land a better version of herself.

They looked up at her, as they always have.

She had forgotten that she is their sky.

The Wonderer

A made woman no doubt, by her own definition.
All of the milestones she pined for, cried for, laid
her life on the line for, she now had. Her greatest
achievements walked around her lounge room and
rested their heads on her shoulder. She wondered
what need she ache for now.
She wondered, after everything she had found,
why she felt so lost.

All The Things

She thought that they were separate: *Her roles.*

She thought that she could break away

and act out each one

independently,

differentially.

She thought that when she was at work, she was the worker

with her child, the mother,

her husband, the lover

herself, the drinker.

But as she hugged her son to her hip,

kissed her husband on the lips,

checked her roster and poured another wine,

she realised she was everything,

all the time.

She was the definition of all but fought the urge to be defined by any.

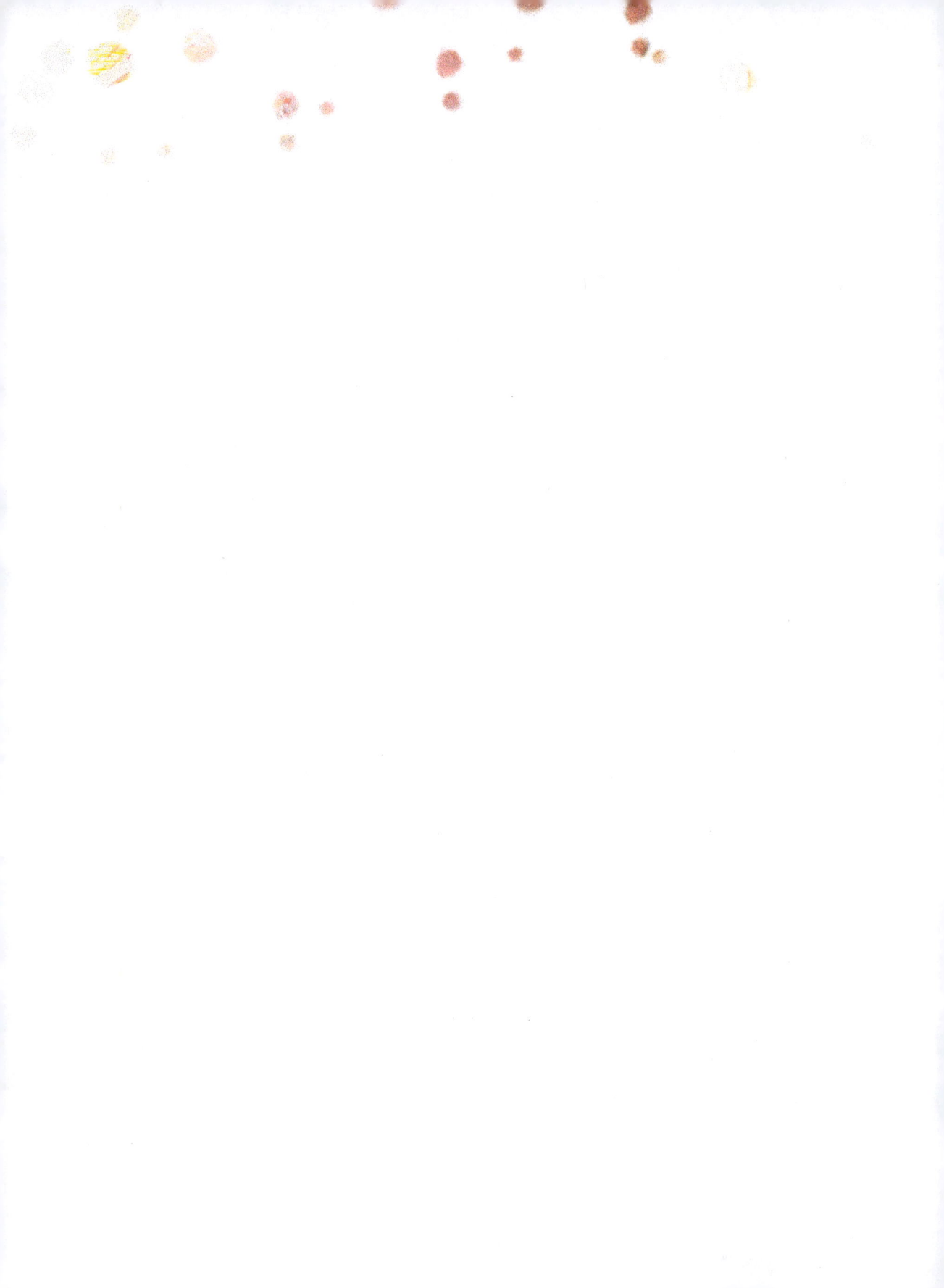

Fuel

The fumes of routine kept the cogs turning and the belts running.

But with nowhere to be,

no strings pulling her limbs to the needy,

she fell in a heap;

threads weaved into blankets, leaving her to sleep.

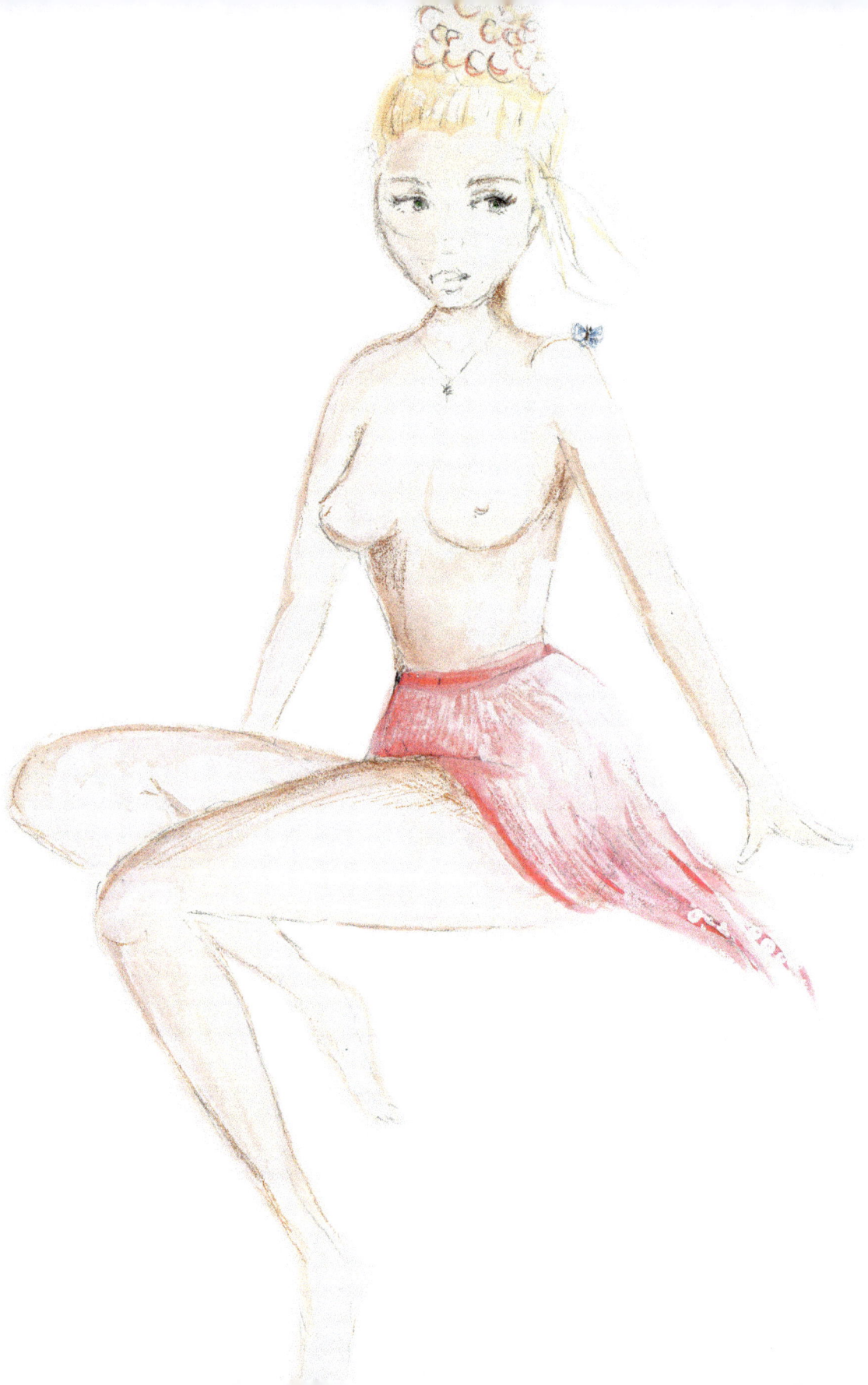

Displaced

Displaced is a word she only learned as an adult and yet
it resonated with her so deeply that when she heard it,
she felt placed.

Wonder

She had ticked all the boxes,

society would be proud.

Studied,

wed,

bred and kept a clean reputation;

she now wondered what was left.

She wondered what else she loved, besides those that needed her.

She wondered what it was she needed to love herself.

Dawn

She drapes herself in glass windows, letting her skin peer out.
The sun warms on the sills and she bakes in the glory of her
natural light.

She is today.

Running

She took up running

not to

not from

but for

herself.

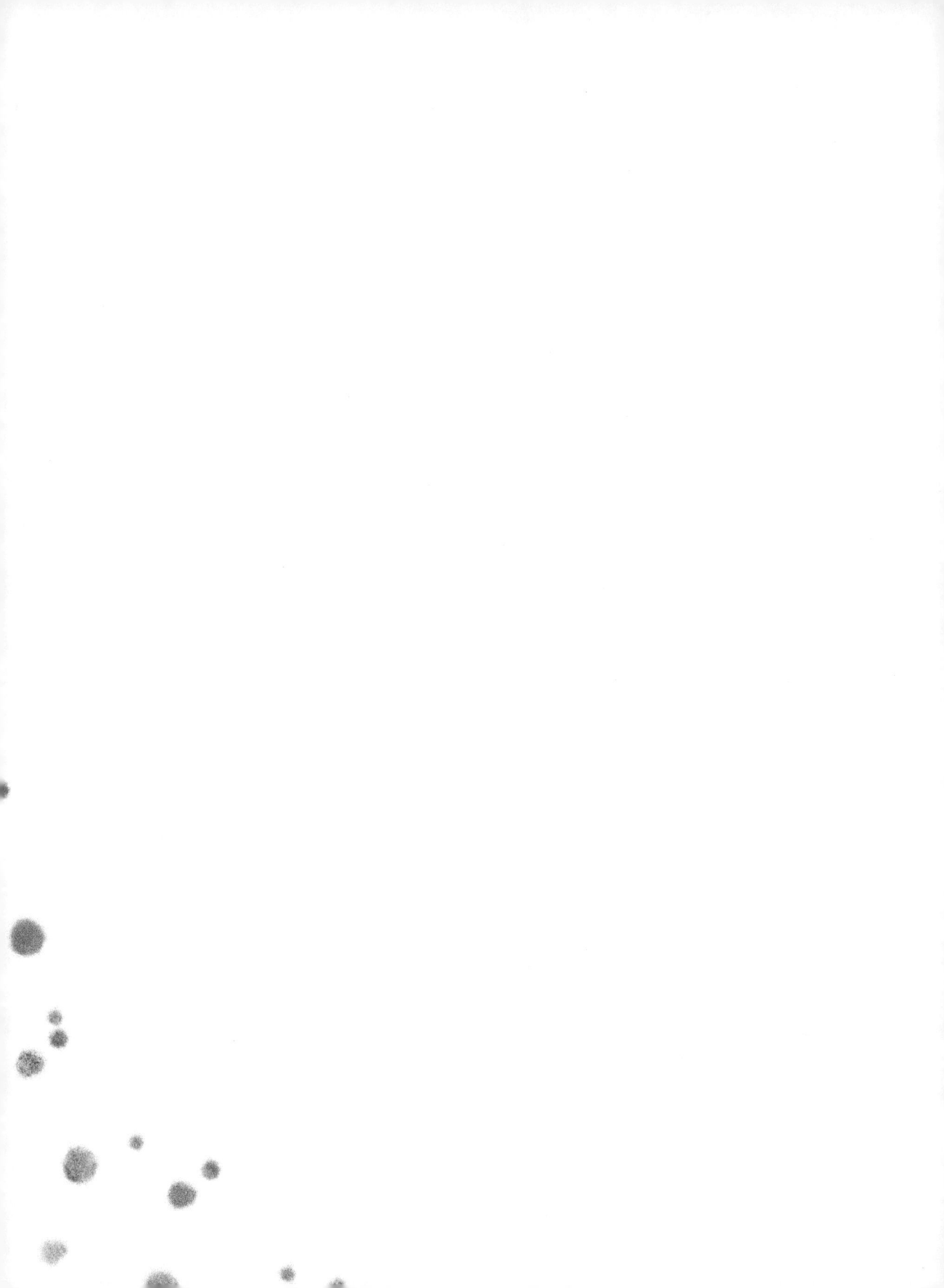

Clay

She finally had time to find herself
after having spent years
unknowingly
creating herself.

Got the look

She wrapped a scarf of blue winter around her hair,

looped her lobes with golden sun

and kissed the mirror with warm blood.

She winked,

a smirk in her crow's feet

and a dare in her flare.

She looked like a rainbow.

Undeniably she was the pot of gold.

All
Out

Twisting of delicate wrists,

the swing of her hips

and, grind in her grooves

she sheds the insecurities of her teenage years

and the shame and desperation of her twenties.

Rebirthed into her truest self

as glances shower her with confidence

she unfolds

under a disco ball.

She lets her hair fall.

She leaves it all on the dance floor.

Strut

Maybe she walks the line,

toes it,

twists it,

fumbles over it in a less than dignified fashion.

She comes out on top.

Scraped knees and no regrets she pleads the fifth.

Her actions strut alongside her and smirk at the smarms.

Judgments fall off her shoulders like dead feathers to a bird.

She cackles, you cannot stop her.

She is not finished yet.

She is not finished yet...

About the Author

TIARE SNOW

From renowned Australian blogger, of *Fly In My Wine*, and author, Tiare Snow delivers a collection of clever, original and moving pieces for women everywhere.

Tiare (pronounced *Ti-ar-dee*) is driven by deeper conversations and observations of the world around her, that is around all of us. She writes about modern motherhood, challenging moments, newfound freedoms, love and inspiration.

A mother of two, wife, fulltime mine site worker and creative writing student, Tiare has been published in multiple online and print journals including *When Women Waken* and *The Vine Leaves Journal.*

Connect with Tiare:

flyinmywine.com & tiaresnow.com

facebook.com/Flyinmywine

instagram.com/flyinmywine

www.ingramcontent.com/pod-product-compliance
Lightning Source LLC
Chambersburg PA
CBHW060755150426
42811CB00058B/1417